Celebrating the Trinity

Faith, Worship and Mission

Myra Blyth

Deputy General Secretary,
Baptist Union of Great Britain

GROVE BOOKS LIMITED
RIDLEY HALL RD CAMBRIDGE CB3 9HU

Contents

The Cover Illustration is by Peter Ashton

First Impression February 2003
ISSN 0262-799X
ISBN 1 85174 523 8

Talking about God
(The Faith of the Church)

1

In a virtual world where spectating is the norm and participating the exception, the Trinity has something of central importance to say about what it is to be alive and human.

To be made in the image of 'One God in Community' is to live in a dynamic relationship with God, with others and with the whole of creation.

Spin doctors by profession play with words, subtly and sometimes deceitfully using them to give the best of possible interpretations to otherwise disastrous events. Their task is to make the truth say what they want it to say. This shadowy activity has contributed to a general cynicism about the trustworthiness of words. Nevertheless, words are a primary tool by which we give shape, definition, meaning and significance to the world around us. By God's Word we were each named into existence.[1] Through words, and more particularly stories, communities come into being and find their identity.

Naming God, however, has always been a tricky matter. Moses was very keen to know God's name, because to know a name is to have power over its bearer. But God would have none of it. In a comical reply to Moses God made clear that any attempt to describe him must remain utterly tentative and provisional: 'I am who I am, I will be who I will be.' It is not that God is unknowable or that anything we can say about God is equally valid or invalid, but that we cannot pin God down. What we can do instead is draw closer to God, using Scripture as a rich resource in which to find words, images, metaphors and analogies appropriate to God. They are there for our benefit, so long as we do not delude ourselves into thinking that words can ever contain the God to whom they refer.

It is not that God is unknowable but that we cannot pin him down

The author of the John's gospel chose his words carefully to reflect on who Jesus was and the nature of his relationship to God. In the gospel, story and theological interpretation are inseparably intertwined:

> The I am sayings, the rich metaphors and images, the poetic language of the prologue, the theological reflections of the farewell discourses and Jesus' repeated statements about his unity with the One who sent him into the world and the repeated identification of God as Jesus' father—all beg the reader to ponder who Jesus is and who God is.[2]

Scholars believe that John's gospel shows many signs of a text that has been worked and re-worked over long years as its author meditated on what Jesus had revealed of God's life to the world, whether they wished to believe in him or not.

The circumstances from which this gospel probably emerged were increasing hostility from the Temple towards the followers of Jesus and a real threat of excommunication. Not surprisingly in this context the gospel sought to present Jesus as both a faithful Jew and radical reformer. Jesus was an orthodox Jew in that he reaffirmed the Jewish confession that 'God is one and besides God there is no other.' But he took a radical step beyond this by stating that he (Jesus) and God (whom he called Abba, Father) were one. In John 14 this *mutual in-dwelling* of the Father and the Son is uncompromisingly presented: 'I am the way and the truth and the life. No one comes to the Father except through me. If you know me, you will know my Father also…whoever has seen me has seen the Father…believe me that I am in the Father and the Father is in me.'

This kind of explicit claim which the fourth gospel attributes to Jesus reflects the evolving awareness within the early Christian community about the nature of God. Yet for all the gospel's sophistication, even here the ideas and the significance of Jesus' life and death were still only taking root. Not in the gospels nor even in the epistles is the threefold nature of God explicitly described. Scripture was very much written in the 'heat of the action.' It offers the unfolding testimony of many whose encounters with the living God in and through the person of Jesus created a mixture of insight, excitement, confusion and martyrdom. The rough and ready testimonies contained in Scripture speak in various ways about God as Father, Son and Spirit, and of the relations between them. The need for the church to teach the faith to enquirers and to defend it against heresy meant that these testimonies were developed into more systematic teaching. By the fifth century the church settled on the formulation of the Trinity that God was of one divine 'nature' in three 'persons,' to guard and point toward the whole witness of Scripture and the full experience of the community of faith. This formulation has stood the test of

The rough and ready testimonies in Scripture speak in various ways about God as Father, Son and Spirit

time, but it is always vulnerable, and needs constantly to be re-appropriated by succeeding generations and cultures.

Functions and Movement

A common tendency at different periods in the history of the church has been to fail to do justice either to the distinctiveness of the three persons (modalism) or conversely to fail to do justice to the unity of God (pluralism). Whilst these heresies were very quickly condemned by the early Fathers, nevertheless they have frequently reappeared at various times in different guises. As Paul Fiddes points out, talks about God the Trinity to children, invariably express 'multiplicity in unity but fail to catch the personal and relational nature.'[3] In *Participating in God*, he cites two examples. The first is a recent occasion of a preacher inviting the children to raise their hands if they had three names. Having been suitably obliged by a number of the children he then proceeded to inform them that God has three names—Father, Son and Holy Spirit. The second example was where a preacher invited the children to think of the persons of the Trinity as different members of the same football team—the manager (the Father), a player (the Son) and the coach (the Holy Spirit). These preachers, notes Fiddes 'have aligned themselves respectively with two historic errors in the development of the doctrine of the Trinity, modalism in the first case and pluralism in the second.'[4]

We are invited somehow not only to know God through his external actions, but to get inside God

Fiddes , along with other recent writers on the Trinity, stresses a way by which these classic problems can be avoided—to concentrate on the dynamic movement between the persons of the Trinity. By this approach the Trinity invites us somehow not only to know God through his external actions, but to get inside God—to know, if you like, a little better what makes God tick! Of course we can never fully *comprehend* God but we can *apprehend* God in the world and in each other even as we move and respond to the rhythm and flow of the Trinity's dance, enjoying its form and pattern, and delighting in its surprising variations.

Attending to the movements within and between the three Persons of the Trinity more than analysing the distinct profiles or functions of the three persons is what can help us as participants in God to live our lives in harmony with the movements that characterize the inner life of God.

To speak of God beyond, beside and within, is not so much a way of describing the persons of God, or even the functions of God, as it is a way of expressing the movement and relations within God. Life as God would have it for us shares these movements.

The freedom or otherness of God is not only a way of marking the distance between us and God, but also points to the importance of distinctness, difference and even separation within God. The Father, Son and Holy Spirit keep a safe distance; they do not collapse into one another but mutually coinhere. In our own experience of living in relationships, it is important that people do not surrender their identities to another. Genuine love does not seek to obliterate the other but to cherish connection and respect freedom. Relationships in which individuals lose a sense of who they are, are emotionally and psychologically damaging. To be a person in the image of God means to have a distinct identity, personality and vocation all of which are realized in relationship.

The solidarity or closeness of God is a way of acknowledging the movement towards the other within the Trinity and out towards the world in creation and redemption. It points to the necessity in relationships for solidarity, empathy and mutuality. Competition and aggression do not make good travelling companions. True community is passionate for justice and deeply unsettled by its absence. The absence of gentleness and the idolization of 'in-your-face' aggression is a scar on the face of humanity. As we move towards each other in love and compassion we lean on the movements of God, who emptied himself of all but love for the sake of the world.

The creativity or energy of God points to the potential in all relationships for a sense of well-being, completeness and wholeness. Such hopes are realized not through the safety of inaction, but by way of risk and vulnerability. By exploring and participating in the full height and depths of human existence we will see the glory of God radiating through the world and reflecting in the face of the other.

Scripture Testifies to God's Freedom and Otherness

God's glory is beyond our finite comprehension. God is mystery. The psalmist tries to fathom the height and depths of this mystery but is quickly defeated. He has no words save wonder and awe. The ancient hymns of the church likewise resort to what is known as 'apophatic' (negative) language in an effort to acknowledge the limitless scope of the Divine One.

> Immortal Invisible God only wise
> In light inaccessible hid from our eyes
> Most blessed most glorious, the ancient of days
> Almighty, victorious, thy great name we praise.

The mystery surrounding God's holiness is stretched further with the realization that whilst God's otherness is sometimes about distance and inaccessibility, it is also and equally about depth and relatedness. God *is* community. God knows and relates to God's self in community and it has always been thus since the beginning of time. In Genesis 1.24 the author invites us to eavesdrop on a conversation going on, as Christians would see it, within the Godhead.

> And God said, 'let us make humans in our own image'…so male and female he created them…and God saw that it was very good.
>
> (Gen 1.26–31)

This text has ancient origins, but within the Christian tradition it has been understood to reveal the plurality and diversity within the heart of God. God is not a singular entity but plural community!

Perhaps more revealing still are the OT Scriptures which speak of wisdom as a distinct agency operative with God in creating the world. Having this character and importance it is not surprising that the wisdom of God is explicitly linked as one and the same with the *logos*, the incarnate Christ, by NT writers.

These biblical allusions to the mystery of God's holiness, and particularly to the relatedness of God's being, lead to the claim—contrary to 21st century virtual reality—that to be made in the image of God, to be truly human, means to live in relationship, to be an engaged participant. Life is not a spectator sport.

To be made in the image of God means to live in relationship

Scripture Testifies to God's Solidarity

We also read in Scripture that the Word eternally begotten of the Father stretches out in empathy and solidarity with humanity sharing its joys and its sorrows. Philippians 2 contains the text of one of the earliest hymns of the church. It reveals the profound theological understanding and insight of the early church, which with the prologue of John's gospel contributed to the teaching of Jesus being co-eternal with the Father, one in being with him, but distinct in his person. Here, as in Genesis 1, the plurality and diversity within God is affirmed, but this time the point is made through emphasizing the distinct mission of God the Son, stretched out across time and eternity equally at work with God in creation and redemption. The text reads, 'counting equality with God not something to be grasped, Christ emptied himself of all but love, and took upon himself the form of a slave.' The second person of the Trinity is not limited to incarnation history, but is already evident in the Old Testament where God suffers and celebrates with his people.

> The drama of brokenness and restoration is shared by Judaism and Christianity. It is a drama of exile and homecoming, death and resurrection, pit and rescue, chaos and creation.[5]

The passages in Isaiah which speak of the suffering servant illustrate well this wider perspective within which the mission of the Son can be appreciated. The message of Isaiah 40–55 is not simply a lofty vision about deliverance from captivity, but a recognition that through its suffering Israel would witness to the good news of the kingdom of Yahweh and this news would reach the ends of the earth. The servant figure is not simply a future reference by Isaiah to the coming of Christ, but is also a reference in the present tense to the day and generation in which he was living.[6] The second person of the Trinity is constantly acting in history, suffering in solidarity with humankind, in order that the good news of God's deliverance will be available to all. The four servant poems (Isaiah 40–55) depict the unusual character of the servant's task both in the turbulent days of Isaiah's ministry and in the days of Christ's sojourn on earth. What is common to all situations is the extraordinary servant methodology:[7]

> A bruised reed he will not break,
>   and a dimly burning wick he will not quench,
> but quietly, gently he will persist
>   until he has established justice in all the earth. (Is 42.3)

The non-violent approach of the suffering servant stands within a great mass of biblical literature which speaks about God's desire to put an end to violent means. Though the NT writers saw Jesus' violent death as announcing the end to the sacrificial system, the logic of violence and retribution undergirds contemporary social and judicial structures throughout the world. The popular appeal for vengeance and sacrifice today seems stronger than ever. The naming, shaming and public pillorying of individuals has become an abiding preoccupation of the tabloid press in response to the insatiable hunger of the masses for a scapegoat.

The popular appeal for vengeance and sacrifice today seems stronger than ever

A newspaper article recently noted the staggering box office appeal in the British gallery-going public for blood. The headline read: 'Galleries tap rich vein of public's lust for blood…gore means more as the macabre Body World Exhibition pulls in the crowds.'[8]

As the martyr bishop Oscar Romero once said to some weeping villagers, who were distressed by the fact that thieves had broken into their church and thrown the reserved sacraments on the ground, 'Why are you so upset by this? Do you not know that the body and blood of Christ is trampled into the mud every day?'

The numbness within us towards the violence and suffering around us means that our solidarity with the innocent victim is exceptional rather than normative. God the Word, however, always remains in solidarity with us and never more so than as the innocent victim whom we seek to destroy.

Scripture Testifies to God's Creativity and Energy

The eternal mission of God's Spirit is to breathe life and possibilities into every situation. The most profound expression of the Creator Spirit is the mighty wind that swept over the waters of the deep. This movement of wind like the fluttering of wings hovered and brooded equally over the waters of creation as well as over the young virgin, ardently eager to create. This was and is the irresistible will for communion, characteristic of God's 'go–between Spirit.'[9] The Spirit comes not only in the wind but also in the fire, pronouncing God's sovereignty over all other powers and gods (Mount Carmel) causing hearts to burn for truth (Emmaus), and raising up voices in ecstatic prayer and praise (Pentecost).

The two NT themes of baptism and Pentecost, represented by water and fire, are themselves strongly suggestive of God's creative energy. They represent the work of the Spirit of God in the life of the individual believer and in the people of God as a whole. It is in the waters of baptism that we not only experience the death of old ways of living, but we are also born into the new resurrection life of Christ (Rom 6.4)—we become part of God's act of new creation (2 Cor 5.17). In a similar way, Pentecost is often referred to by Christians as the 'birthday of the church,' the time when the Spirit brought into being a new people of God. It is this new people who have been called out of darkness into light, from not being into being (1 Peter 2.9–10).

Naturally in the excitement and confusion of the resurrection period significant reflection about the nature of God did not easily take place. Cool dispassionate theology is not the stuff of revolution! Nevertheless just as the shy person of the Trinity, the Holy Spirit, constantly points away from self preferring to highlight the other persons of the Trinity so the testimonies of Jesus' followers point us faithfully Godwards yielding up, little by little, a distinctive shape and pattern which given time and reflection has emerged as One God, Father, Son and Holy Spirit.

Cool, dispassionate theology is not the stuff of revolution

God Beyond Scripture

Now of course the obvious question is, if Scripture did not get bothered about precise Trinitarian formulations, why on earth should we? Would not Christianity be more accessible, defendable and celebrated today if the looseness and openness of the original testimonies could stand alone from all this history and tradition?

Faith is a living, evolving reality based on a dynamic relationship with the living Word

One answer to this question is to insist that faith is not ahistorical. Faith is a living, evolving reality based on a dynamic relationship with the living Word. A stand-alone approach to Scripture would have the opposite effect to that intended. The church would become a museum, locked in a post-resurrection time warp. The gospel would be stripped of the newness, innovation and spontaneity that makes it a unique source of life and hope in every generation.

A second response to this question is to remind ourselves that in times of persecution an oppressed people need to be able to state clearly and simply what it is that they believe. Moreover, we need to be able to explain the faith in terms understandable to cultures and societies who find the gospel offensive and inconvenient. The early church apologists were missionaries in their own right. They were speaking the good news into the culture of their day, in exactly the way we are called to do in the 21st century. Ironically today, in a pluralist world where Christianity is once again a minority, even though religious sympathies are on the ascendancy, the church is faced with remarkably similar challenges to those faced by 2nd and 3rd century Christian apologists.

The challenge of the Trinity for the ancient reader was to appreciate that the dignity and value ascribed to God could also be associated with persons. According to a platonic view of the universe, persons were of little importance and of no lasting value. The popular Greek tragedies of Plato's day illustrate well the very low value placed on human persons. Whatever limited freedom was enjoyed by humans in these epic dramas always ultimately proved futile. Heroes and heroines alike were hopelessly subjected to the whim of the gods, and invariably ended up as victims of blind fate.[10] Describing God in personal terms then, when persons had no inherent value, was self-evidently foolishness to the Greeks. No wonder Christianity sent shock waves through the learned corridors of Greek civilization.

The writer Steve Turner in a short poem entitled *The History Lesson* offers us a salutary warning: 'History repeats itself. It has to, no-one ever listens…'[11] In other words, rather than ignore the attempts of our ancestors in the faith, perhaps we could exercise a little humility and ask ourselves what we might learn from their efforts to know God and engage in counter-cultural mission. Scripture is full of testimonies which speak variously of experiencing God as Father, Son and Spirit. The early church Fathers tried to describe God in a manner which would correspond with this testimony and it was for this reason they came up with the formulation One God—three persons.

Our faith in a triune God can often feel like the unreconstructed concern of ancient philosophers and theologians. But this need not be. Trinitarian faith draws us towards the central message of the gospel. Alongside the classical question of the rich young ruler 'what must I do to be saved?' Trinitarian faith suggests that a central and prior question to this is 'what does it mean to be human' and related to that 'what value must I place on human life.' These I would suggest are the questions which resonate with contemporary generations and for that reason should be our starting point and our *raison d'être* in mission.

Identity and Diversity

Our present confusion about human identity and value is well illustrated by the headline manner in which we treat the subject of genetic technology. In the twinkling of an eye, or more exactly in the flash of one news story across the world's TV channels, the first claim to human cloning brought fame and notoriety to a freak religious group (the Raelians). Their identity and beliefs would not have caught the attention of the world without the attendant claim to having uncovered the secret formula by which to create and control life. Just three years ago, legislation went through the Westminster parliament to ensure that genetic research would not progress from cloning animals to cloning humans. The fear generated by this subject in the public was furnished by horror images of crazy dictators trying to secure the pure and perfect race. Around about the same time as this story was prominent, but unrelated to it, a meeting between a group of artists took place, including the composer James McMillan and the now Archbishop Rowan Williams. In the course of their discussions this subject of genetic engineering took on some importance.

The primary difficulty for modern readers in the Western world is that we automatically think of three individuals

After many reflections together a project was begun to produce a musical dramatization called Parthenogenesis. It is a curious story from wartime Berlin, of a woman who apparently gave birth to a girl by immaculate conception. Rowan Williams recalls how this story provides a negative or reverse image of the annunciation, for what the woman conceived was not wholly other but utterly the same.[12] It is a story that raises fundamental questions about our fascination with genetic control and our pathological interest in genetic sameness and stability. What, Williams asks, does the cult of sameness and repetition do to love, and ultimately to growth and movement in real history?

It is urgent, given the ethical maze we are in, to try to unpack how faith in God the Trinity can help contemporary generations respond to this core question about human identity and existence.

The primary difficulty for modern readers looking at Trinitarian language in the western world is that when we speak of God as three persons we automatically think of three individuals. Millions of people live life in the 21st century as isolated individuals and consider competition, ambition and individual achievement to be the secret of human fulfilment. In such a cultural context it follows that the notion of God as three persons does not naturally lead to the impression 'One God in community.'

When, by contrast, this language was used by the Cappadocian Fathers[13] in 4th and 5th century Greece the word 'person' could never have been understood to mean an isolated individual. To be a person was to be in relationship. One God in three persons was a picture of a community of mutual and reciprocal relationship.

If we could recover the vision of 'persons-in-relationship' as we see it expressed in the movements within God, then we might begin to see how Trinitarian language is radically counter-cultural. To be made in the image of God means to live as persons in community. Trinitarian language alters the logic and with it the grammatical infrastructure of our lives. In response to the Trinity we renounce the 'I–me' world preferring instead to speak more generously and more dynamically in terms of 'I–thou' and 'we–us.'

At the core of what it means to be human and fulfilled is a call to 'live with and for others rather than self'

The challenge of Trinity for the modern reader is to appreciate that at the core of what it means to be human and fulfilled is a call to 'live with and for others rather than self' and to celebrate otherness rather than to try to control and eliminate it.

The common overriding challenge presented by the language of One God in community, to ancient and postmodern cultures alike, is to stop talking about God and the world as if we were distant spectators and begin to engage with God and each other as in a committed relationship.[14]

Communicating with God (The Worship of the Church) 2

In an eclectic world, where art and spirituality are a mix-and-match affair, worship can easily be a potent cocktail of dubious content.

Nevertheless the arts are uniquely placed in this post-literate era to enable us to appreciate and worship God as Trinity and to develop a practical and Trinitarian approach to worship.

Trinitarian worship is not simply about reciting a threefold formula, but celebrating the story of God's saving acts in history, and discovering our place in the unfolding events. This is an epic drama which explores the timeless themes of Genesis to Revelation.

It is in worship that most people today are aware, superficially at least, of the doctrine of the Trinity. We sing hymns that address the three persons in the Godhead, we invoke the presence of the triune God, glorify God the Trinity at various points and pray to the Father through the Son in the Spirit.

Because Christian formation takes place almost exclusively for many people in the context of public worship, it is incredibly important for those preparing and leading worship to try to nurture Trinitarian shapes and patterns in all that is done.

Music

Many churches throughout the country, regardless of denominational character, draw extensively from contemporary renewal songs. Hymnbooks have taken second place to the OHP. The song repertoire of a local church is a very eclectic and random selection drawn from an enormous range of sources. Songs find their way onto the list more because they are popular to sing than because they might help to fill out the range of themes and possibilities that music in worship should cover.

Much time could usefully be spent in churches analysing the types of songs that are most often sung and the function these songs fulfil in the worship. Michael Hawn, in an article entitled 'Form and Ritual,' reminds

Songs find their way onto the list more because they are popular to sing

us that music for singing within worship is structured to fulfil a variety of different functions.[15] Some songs are *informational* and others *transformational*. Informational songs are sequential in form. Hymns are typically informational where an idea or storyline progresses through the verses covering the story of God's activity in the creation and redemption of the world. With each verse the story builds to a climax concluding with a doxological affirmation of the mystery of the Triune God. For many generations this form of singing has been the primary means of learning about the faith. It has a strong didactic function. Though this type of music is less popular in worship at the moment, modern hymnwriters continue to produce texts using their poetic imagination to express the gospel and to explore ancient truths about God in ways appropriate to the current world. Take for example the communion hymn *Great God, your love has called us here* by Brian Wren. In scope it is thoroughly Trinitarian, and in mood there is a sympathetic juxtaposition of suffering (both human and divine) with the hope of healing and life through the sharing of bread and wine. It includes these verses:

> Great God, your love has called us here
> as we, by love, for love were made.
> Your living likeness still we bear,
> though marred, dishonoured, disobeyed.
> We come, with all our heart and mind
> your call to hear, your love to find.
>
> We come with self-inflicted pains
> of broken trust and chosen wrong,
> half free, half bound by inner chains,
> by social forces swept along.
> We strain to glimpse your mercy seat
> and find you kneeling at our feet.[16]

More recently singer/songwriters from the charismatic movement such as Graham Kendrick are developing songs which are exploring more fully the range of topics and emotions that a rigorous Trinitarian approach invites:

> For the joys and the sorrows—the best and the worst times
> For this moment for tomorrow, for all that lies behind
> Fears that crowd around me, for the failure of my plans
> For the dreams of all I hope to be, the truth of what I am
>
> For this I have Jesus…[17]

More and more, Kendrick is seen to be moving beyond his traditional genre, offering in contemporary style an eloquent expression of the experience of suffering and doubt. Such songs, however, are not yet numerous. Recent research shows that mainstream hymnbooks right across the range consistently divide their material across four main themes.[18] But there is a striking contrast here with the more recent *Songs of Fellowship* and music published by Vineyard:

Theme	Mainstream	SofF	Vineyard
Human suffering and doubt	11%	2%	2%
Praise and celebration	30%	60%	30%
Discipleship and social justice	30%	13%	1%
Intimacy and devotion	29%	25%	67%

The study argues that renewal music in the UK and the USA is guilty of neglecting the negative aspects of human experience in worship. This is not the case with renewal music in mainstream Europe and was not the case in the music of early Pentecostalism where renewal worship has its roots.

'Where is the lamentation?' was Bishop Graham Cray's challenge recently to the worship leaders at Sole Survivor, Britain's latest and fastest growing renewal gathering. Variety of course does not come by simply creating a melange of different styles, but by every writer having the integrity within their own distinctive style to embrace a diversity of themes and ideas which do justice to the diversity of God.

Ironically, whilst churches may not be using their hymnbooks much these days, they would be well advised not to throw them away for the treasures therein are even now being rediscovered and incorporated in contemporary worship settings. In typically postmodern fashion, hymns of the church are being unashamedly borrowed, adapted and re-invented so that Trinitarian poetry is powerfully re-entering contemporary worship spaces. Some of the contenders for this postmodern hymn renaissance include beautiful Trinitarian hymns such as *Be Thou My Vision* and *Holy*.

The function of transformational music is to sustain and carry ideas already introduced in the liturgy

The other most common musical structure used within worship takes the form of short cyclic/repetitive songs and chants. John Bell calls this transformational music because its function is not to inform the faith, but to sustain and carry ideas already introduced at key points in the liturgy such as the readings, prayers, sermon, and the Eucharist. These songs help the worshipper to hold on to or focus on an idea which gently takes root in hearts and minds.

Michael Hawn recalls how he became aware of the power of cyclic forms of music during his first visit to the Taizé Community in south-eastern France.[19] At first the brief texts, endlessly repeated, seemed like sheer redundancy, but after a time he sensed that repetition was not an accurate description of this musical experience. The theme kept returning. Rather than redundancy the experience was replete with variations. Some time later whilst teaching in Africa, he again encountered this form of theme and variation. As in Taizé, he found the African liturgies used shorter musical forms, with less textual content than the hymns from his own tradition. But the African musical style was radically different to the generally meditative sung prayers of Taizé. The interplay of call and response, the subtle use of percussion, the rhythmic dance which accompanied the singing and the intensity which seemed to gather with each recurrence of the theme made for a very distinctive experience.

Cyclic songs and chants subtly bring us into an experience of God's mysterious threefold presence

The variations in the rhythm, timbre, tone and mood of worship songs and chants often reflects the distinctive character of particular contexts and cultures, as well as the particular insights of worshipping communities where the music emerged. By sharing short cyclical songs across countries, continents and centuries the universal church invites the church locally to expand faith and horizons in the God who made us and nurtures us. For example, the chant *Kyrie Eleison* (Lord, have mercy) means the same thing wherever it is sung but the variations in how this is sung are crucial. Russian, Celtic, Caribbean *Kyries* by dint of their distinctive rhythms and sounds expose us to different aspects of God's mercy. Equally the *Sanctus* (Holy, holy ,holy) is a universal chant, but the *Sanctus* sung by Latin Americans, or Greeks or Africans will open us in very different ways to the mystery of God's holiness.

Whilst sequential song and hymn texts overtly describe the mysteries of the triune God and ascribe the honour due to God, cyclic songs and chants subtly bring us into an experience of God's mysterious threefold presence through the musical journey of theme and variation. Whereas in formal logic and philosophy the categories of oneness and difference are rigidly separated and mutually exclusive, in music we find an alternative conceptual space. In polyphonic music where theme and variation is a fundamental preoccupation,

> the addition of new contrapuntal themes does not obliterate or even necessarily diminish the significance of the themes already in place. In this sense music is a metaphor for understanding the mystery of One God, three persons. Attention to any one of the three does not

need to imply a demised role for the others. All three have their distinctive melodies and all are heard and played simultaneously without damage to God's unity.[20]

Trinity may be foreign to the language and logic of arithmetic and philosophy but not to music. The pastoral and theological challenge facing all those with responsibility for music in worship is to ensure that the musical forms as well as the content and style they choose will enable worshippers to enter into a rich and diverse experience of the triune God. Music in worship should enable the full range of emotions to find expression. This of course is not easy when power and success are the primary indicators for human well-being. It is disturbing to see how the common and all-pervading idea which runs through many charismatic renewal songs is a fascination with God's power. We have become the children of an upfront, in-your-face, football terrace God. Worship needs to embrace a wider range of human emotions such as suffering, pain, vulnerability, generosity and mutuality. We need more of the light-and-shade subtlety and variety that belongs to the triune God.

Trinity may be foreign to the language and logic or arithmetic and philosophy but not to music

Prayer

The prayer life of a congregation is often where muddled thinking about God the Trinity appears. To whom, exactly, are we praying?

The passages in the New Testament that distinguish most clearly between the Father, the Son and the Holy Spirit are those which deal with prayer. Christ as our reconciler and peace-giver is the one through whom 'we have access by one spirit to the Father' (Eph 2.18). Whilst all three persons of the Trinity are involved in our communion with God, it is normally to the Father that the Son and Spirit lead us in prayer.[21]

Jesus teaches us when we pray to address God as Abba, a tender but respectful term for Father, thereby assuming our status as God's adopted children. It is significant that the pronoun used in the Lord's Prayer is not *my* Father but *our* Father. Just as the God whom we worship is three persons in community, so the prayers we offer in worship are the prayers of the community. The language of 'I and me' belongs to the selfish vocabulary of a fragmented and egotistical world. The language of 'we and us' gathers us into the inner life of the triune God; it is the language of heaven.

The objections raised in recent years to a strict adherence to gender specific language fall into two categories. The first objection arises from the emotional difficulties many people have in using a term like 'father' to address

God. The growing awareness of child abuse, and particularly concerning the sexual exploitation of children by their fathers or even priests renders useless such metaphors as loving father. Of course it can be rightly argued that God is not our Father in the same sense as we know human fathers; it is an analogy and moreover it is a positive description of fatherhood as God would have us experience it. But this reasoning is of little consolation to those who have been and wounded physically and emotionally.

The second objection comes from theologians who believe that strict adherence to gender specific language gives to first century culture and its patriarchal social infrastructure and customs a normative position which we would not insist on in other culturally specific readings of the NT. The argument follows that Jesus' way was always to break down the barriers of gender, race and class, emphasizing that we are all one in Christ, and that in Christ there is neither male nor female. Such a radical redefining of our status before God needs at least to be matched by overt recognition within worship and prayer that God in essence is not male but beyond gender.

Many on both ends of the argument are not content with a balancing act

The compromise line in this debate in many local situations is to allow traditional male metaphors like Father, King, and Lord to be complemented by other more feminine biblical metaphors for God such as mother, or wisdom. Many on both ends of this argument, however, are not content with a balancing act. Geoffrey Wainwright insists that it is not a question of giving equal status to all metaphorical language. Some metaphors simply illustrate God's attitude towards people and the world; other metaphors such as the Father-Son relationship are 'highly privileged' metaphors and carry the status of 'primary language.' On this basis he insists that 'the historic identity of the Christian faith is at stake if that structure is obscured or the best name we have is abandoned.'[22] In contrast to this, feminist theologians Ruth Duck and Patricia Wilson Kastner argue that precisely because metaphorical language points to a reality beyond what is described, there is every reason to explore the full range of metaphors that Scripture and tradition can offer us. They note how many during the 1990s found inspiration in the wisdom literature within Scripture, because here was a feminine metaphor of God which identified God in roles not traditionally assigned to women, such as creator, architect, eternal One. But their primary plea is for theological and historical humility:

Our task today is to build on the critical insights the church gained at great cost from the early Trinitarian controversies and (like our forebears) as we analyse Trinitarian language in the interest of fuller praise,

> we must seek by whatever metaphors we use, to speak about God the Trinity in terms of coequality among the partners rather than subordination of one to another and to recognize the distinctiveness of each partner rather than blurring the identities.[23]

Debates about the language we use in prayer to address God can obscure that fact that prayer is not primarily our activity. It is rather God's gift to us through Christ and the Holy Spirit. Spiritual directors, with biblical precedent, are at pains to emphasize how prayer is more about listening intently than talking incessantly.

What is it that Christians who attend silently to God discover? First attempts at attending silently to God often result in darkness, obscurity and distraction. The moments lack content, but gradually amidst the obscurity it dawns on the

Prayer is more about listening intently than talking incessantly

person praying that this activity is actually the activity of another. It is the experience of being prayed in, the discovery that 'we do not know how to pray, as we ought' (Rom 8) but are graciously caught up in a divine conversation which is passing back and forth in and through the one who prays. In our weakness and inarticulacy divine dialogue flows.[24]

One of the most ancient ways by which worshippers have sought to pray and to enter more deeply into the mysteries of the triune God has been with the accompaniment of icons. Today after centuries when the icon tradition was neglected and even rejected, there is widespread interest again.

One of the most famous and celebrated icons of all time is Andrei Rublev's painting of the Holy Trinity. This icon expresses in silence aspects of God which words struggle to express. The picture depicts the OT scene where Abraham and Sarah are visited by three angelic beings under the oaks of Mamre. They give the strangers hospitality and in the course of the meal learn that they will soon bear a son. The early Christian church recognized in this scene a revelation of the Holy Trinity, a communion of three persons as One God.

> Apart from the colour of the clothing the three figures are identical. Each head is submissively inclined toward one of the others, none of the three assumes an imperial attitude. There is an atmosphere of love, freedom, rest and intimate communion. The sense of oneness is achieved primarily through the gentle attentive engagement of the three with each other, the joining of eyes. Due to inverse perspective the icon has no vanishing point. The three figures are not part of a disappearing plane but rather seem to move ever closer to the person

viewing the icon. The effect of inverse perspective attracts us, drawing us towards the table and thus towards eucharistic life. This most celebrated representation of the Trinity enjoys enormous popularity far beyond Orthodoxy because it attracts and invites the worshipper to share in the divine life.[25]

Whilst greater attentiveness in our singing and praying to the nature of God as three persons in community can serve to enrich worship, our songs and prayers do not in themselves take us to the heart of what is meant by the phrase Trinitarian worship. Songs and prayers, like Trinitarian 'gestures,' are a helpful and disciplined way of constantly keeping the big picture of God's saving actions firmly in focus, but they do not provide that overarching framework or momentum which allows the different parts to coinhere and which enables worship to be in its totality Trinitarian. For this we need to look deeper.

Movement

Worship in Isaiah 6 is about being caught up into the worship of heaven. The prophet's experience in the Temple is multi-sensory and all-consuming. He hears and is drawn into the angels' brilliant antiphonal hymn of praise celebrating the glory of God and acknowledging the awesome power of God's presence. He smells the incense rising up in sweet praise and feels the call of God on his life to rise up and serve. But the moment is too much. Instead of feeling the joy of God's invitation, he is overcome by his own sense of distance from God and from himself. The prophet feels he has no place in God's plan, for in contrast to the glory of that worship, his life is inadequate and unremarkable. The touch of the hot coals cleansing his lips and his life transform the experience from distant observer to engaged participant. Isaiah joins the chorus of the angels and starts to locate himself within God's story.

My first experience of worship in the Orthodox tradition was in the Russian Orthodox Cathedral in Moscow in 1982. In my *naiveté* I felt like I was observing and experiencing something akin to a grand opera production. The music was as brilliant as the angel's chorus in Isaiah 6. It soared to the heights of the great dome above us, resonating in that spherical space as if the whole earth was fit to burst out in praise. The movements of the clergy and the attentiveness of the packed congregation was all quite mystifying, but the overall sense of being caught up into something quite mysterious and marvellous was intensely worshipful.

Alexander Schmemann, a great teacher of the Orthodox faith, has done much to open Western eyes and ears to the meaning and purpose within the Orthodox liturgy. In his book *For the Life of the World*, he has pleaded that the heart of worship is the Eucharist (Communion), for here we enter into the joy of God, and from here we witness to Jesus Christ the source of life for the world.[26]

Schmemann takes the reader through the liturgy step by step. His purpose is to show that worship as a whole is sacramental, and not just some elements within it. Worship is one transforming act, one ascending movement. And the goal of this movement of ascension is to take us out of this world and to make us partakers of the world to come.

Worship as a whole is sacramental, not just some elements within it

In pleading for a eucharistic focus in worship Schmemann is not thinking exclusively of the events of passion week, but is envisaging more broadly and symbolically the total mission of God, Father, Son and Holy Spirit. He is envisaging on the scale of a grand opera the whole story of creation and redemption unfolding in glorious technicolor.

Worship begins a journey or procession into the life of the risen Christ. This is not about escaping from the world, but arriving at a vantage point where we can see more deeply into the reality of the world. Only by leaving and ascending can we enjoy the transforming power and reality of God's kingdom. This was the experience of the disciples who ascended the mount with Jesus. This movement towards God symbolically underlines the intended destination of all humanity and is announced and sealed by the opening doxology 'Blessed is the Kingdom of the Father, the Son and the Holy Spirit now and ever unto ages of ages, Amen.'

Critical of western theologians who 'instead of following the order of the eucharistic journey with its progressive revelation of meaning, have applied to the Eucharist a set of abstract questions,' Schmemann argues that

> This approach squeezes out interest in the liturgy itself and what remains are isolated moments, formulas and conditions of validity. What disappears is the Eucharist as one organic all-embracing and all-transforming act of the whole church and what remains are essential and non-essential parts, elements and consecration.[27]

The attraction of the eucharistic journey as described by Schmemann is that all the parts coinhere in an overarching movement of ascension. As the movement of journey progresses we symbolically rehearse the story of God's gracious love towards the world, every step of the way positioning ourselves before God physically and spiritually in ways appropriate to the moments within the story. All this of course may sound a touch exotic (especially to my Baptist friends!) so let me try to recast the language of eucharistic journey into a more free church or evangelical discourse.

Music, prayer, art and storytelling all assist greatly in the creating of an appropriate climate and context for vibrant worship. And yet worship is more than the sum of its parts. It is a total experience, in which the overarching movements and shape echo the movements of freedom, solidarity and energy within the triune God. Whilst the Orthodox describe this movement in terms of a eucharistic journey, my own tradition would speak rather of covenant journey. The Orthodox see it as a journey of ascent into heaven and back again. The Baptists would describe it as the gathering and scattering of God's covenant people in which, through the glorious presence of the Risen and ascended Christ, heaven comes to earth more than the other way around. Despite the real differences in structure and style and even theology, Orthodox and Baptist alike both stress movement, both see journey and hospitality as defining metaphors, and both celebrate worship as the point where heaven and earth meet.

In a recent collection of essays by seven evangelical Anglicans, entitled *Mass Culture,* some striking comments were made about the need for the so-called non-liturgical churches to get serious about the drama and spectacle of worship. The main concern of this group is the mission of the church in a postmodern culture and their conviction is that Communion holds the key. One contributor, Sam Richards, presents the challenge this way,

> The Eucharist tells the gospel story, and it does not leave the listeners and hearers as bystanders or voyeurs but calls them into the story…This preliterate medium (storytelling) may prove to be the most powerful available to Christians in an increasingly post-literate age. Now may be the moment for "new" and traditionally free church traditions to consider exploring the place of liturgy and ritual within their worship so that they are able to offer people ways of participating in the eucharistic story in church. We live in a world that understands spectacle and drama. If we want contemporary culture to come and see we must have something to show them as well as to say.[28]

My point is that worship has a core shape and pattern, which is Trinitarian inspired. Within that there is great scope for theme and variations as well as infinite potential for improvisation in genre and style.

Participating in God (The Mission of the Church) 3

The movements within God (like a divine dance), from Father to Son, and Son to Father, and the mediation of the Spirit constantly opening up fresh possibilities within that relationship, have profound consequences for life as we know it.

Mission is of the essence of God, so our life together in God is about continuing the processions of God by reaching out in love and community, offering healing and hope in the middle of fragmentation and exclusion.

The road to Emmaus recorded in Luke 22 is a eucharistic journey which quickly draws connections between worship and life. In this journey of faith the disciples were helped to see the long-term consequences for them of their relationship with Christ. Just when they thought this phase of their lives was all over they realized that it was only beginning. Cleopas was disturbed because the tomb was empty. He could not bring closure to this chapter of his life, because on top of all that had happened now even the blessed memory of Jesus had been disturbed. In the familiarity of bread and wine, Cleopas realized that this stranger was Jesus but yet this Jesus was not the person of his memory or imagination. This Jesus was other. Though the glory of God is seen in the human suffering of the crucified Jesus (especially in John), the empty tomb and the resurrection challenge us not to reduce God in Christ to the familiar but to extend our sights to the God who is beyond and other than us.[29]

The empty tomb and the resurrection challenge us not to reduce God in Christ to the familiar

The resurrection expands the horizon of faith, and fills the believer with expectation. This was also the experience of the disciples on the road to Emmaus and of the church on the day of Pentecost. It was no New Year party where the hangover would cloud out the experience. This was the beginnings of a living encounter with the Risen Christ, made possible through God's Spirit within them. Jesus was not just a memory to be preserved. God beyond and with them was also powerfully within and among them, and made the prospect of life this side of death a renewed possibility.

John Taylor writes of the church in our day:

> We have lost our nerve and our sense of direction and have turned the divine initiative into a human enterprise…And all these drab infidelities are committed not because too little power is available to us, but because the power so far exceeds the petty scale we want to live by. God has made us a little lower than the angels, while our highest ambition is to live a little above the Joneses. We are looking for a sensible family-sized God dispensing pep pills or tranquillizers as required with a Holy Spirit who is a baby's comforter. No wonder the Lord of terrible aspect is too much for us.[30]

Faith in God, Father, Son and Holy Spirit, is never satisfied simply by talking about God in clever polemics, or even talking to God through beautiful worship. Unless we are prepared to move and live in God, the mystery of the Trinity will always remain on the level of a mathematical conundrum. The movements within God, like a divine dance from Father to Son, and Son to Father, and the mediation of the Spirit constantly opening up fresh possibilities within that relationship, describe the essentially missionary character of the Triune God.[31] Acts 2 is the moment *par excellence* for the early church when the missionary profile of God is especially vivid. The creative and redeeming work of God bursts open once again on to the human scene as the Spirit fills individuals and whole communities to claim life, hope and a future in the face of death and despair.

Within my own church tradition (Baptist) there is a deep sense of the missionary nature of the triune God. The eternal procession of God, creating, redeeming and sustaining the earth speaks powerfully about the self-giving self-sending and self-emptying nature of God. God is by nature ready to risk and to lose. In his own image he made a world that is innovative, surprising, novel and outrageous. God is open, expansive and inclusive. God delights in change. God risks the unimaginable in preference to the predictable and safe. God suffers with and dies for those who are lost preferring the solidarity of the suffering to the isolation of the successful.

God is by nature ready to risk and to lose

The missionary nature of the triune God then is always about breaking the mould; not doing things in one way but many; not insisting on how things are or were, but celebrating the new and untried. This God who makes all things new does not call or ask for commitment to sameness and safety but for an openness to the strange and the miraculous. The future towards which God calls us offers us little in terms of certainty but everything in terms of faith and hope.

Corresponding to this missionary profile, the calling of the church needs to be mission shaped. Like the early followers of Christ the church in the present day needs to break the mould. In Acts 15 we read about a potential showdown between Paul and the church in Jerusalem. The Jerusalem agenda was to preserve and keep pure the faith of God's people. As such Paul's missionary zeal and his maverick ways were a deep irritation. Paul seemed intent on expansion at any price. The long-held traditions and customs of the Jewish faith were being relativized and even discarded on the grounds that the heart of the gospel speaks into every culture rather than being the possession or privilege of any one culture.

Like the early followers of Christ the church in the present day needs to break the mould

In the 6th century these British Isles witnessed a curious parallel to Acts 15. At the Synod of Whitby the leaders of the two streams of church tradition (Roman and Celtic) sought to resolve their differences. On the surface the problems were very ecclesiastical—reconciling church calendars and liturgical attire. But at the root of the dispute lay completely different approaches to organizing church, and with it to understanding God. The Celtic missionaries were 'pilgrims of permanent departure.'[32] They had no feeling for developing highly organized church structures but much passion for planting churches or, more exactly, planting crosses. They thrived on the edges, where communities were simply and loosely knit together and where order was determined by the God-given patterns of seasons and cycles. The Roman church, in contrast, established itself in centres of population and cultural activity. Religion and political life meshed easily, and theology reinforced the more sophisticated political human aspirations for good order. Of course the matter was more complicated than this, but the analogy stands much analysis and corresponds incredibly to the situation we now face again in postmodern Britain.

Today, with decline in mainstream historic Christianity and revival in alternative religious activities, Paul rather than Peter, Antioch more than Rome, the Celts more than the Romans, the provisional and experiential more than the organizational and hierarchical is the missionary priority. When it comes to Trinitarian theology, the Celtic tradition promises a great deal. Its non-hierarchical, communitarian approach to organization may be politically naïve but it is theologically strong. The sensitivity to God's transcendence and otherness fused with God's immanence in all things created lends itself to the poetry of faith more than the conceptualizations of doctrinal truth. The Celtic tradition thrived in an oral, story-based culture. Their passion for the heroes of the faith was carved onto crosses, allowing the epic drama of salvation to be readily rehearsed.

Contemporary cynicism about organized religion, and distrust of centralized structures presents a crisis for the church as an institution, but not for Christianity itself. The mission of the triune God transcends these historical glitches by breaking into cultures in new, surprising and outrageous ways. Historic churches may fear the end of organized religion as we have known it, but not God.

What then is the architecture of a missionary church? Jesus gives us a clue to this in the dramatic scene of the cleansing of the Temple. This was a full frontal attack by the Son of God on organized religion. He was not opposed to the Temple so much as to the orchestrated way in which the religious leadership had ring-fenced sacred space. Access to God was carefully and rigidly defined, denying the impure and unchosen any right of access. Their crime was to violate the awesome simplicity of holy ground. Today's church needs to be accessible to more people, and that means transforming our notions of church as a place. Public space is holy ground and may be a more conducive environment for religious experience than traditional religious places. Ground Zero, the land once occupied by the twin towers, has become a place of pilgrimage. People go there to search through the rubble of their lives, to ask questions that the normal round of business as usual does not permit. This land which once cradled the icons of world capitalism has become holy ground.

In a similar way, prayers on the common of a housing estate to remember the victims and perpetrators of a local murder incident, were initiated by a local Baptist minister and three of his congregation. Their vigil brought the community out of their houses and onto the green, some just leaning out of windows, others wandering as far as the garden fence, others still more curious came closer and joined the group. At the end locals applauded the move. 'That was great!' they said to the minister, 'you must come again.' What the minister and members realized more truly than ever was how much God is out there in the community whilst they are hiding in the church.

Hospitality is being rediscovered as a primary metaphor for church

Efforts by churches of all traditions to expand the space has resulted in pubs, clubs and virtual worlds being claimed as missionary territory. Visit cyber space, enter the clubbers' church and touch a way of doing church which does not correspond to normal definitions. Hospitality is being rediscovered as a primary metaphor for church.[33] Luke's Gospel is set within the frame of eight scenes of hospitality meals. This is the rationale behind the buying up of pubs, as well as the genius behind the *Alpha* courses. Eating and drinking together, once central to the identity of the church, has become sanitized self-conscious activity, reduced to eucharistic formulas which often offer little by way of nourishment, either physical or spiritual. New ways of doing church might appear to be a world away from Schmemann's eucharistic liturgy, but they are in fact appropriating the heart of the movement that he is arguing for.

Conclusion

In this booklet we have explored ways of talking about God. We have chosen words which are more relational than dogmatic, more provisional than absolute. By this means our hope is to glimpse the holiness of God, not to control the mystery of God.

At the same time as grappling with God talk, this booklet has also explored the question, what does it mean to be human? In the current culture, where human identity and value is often cheap and dispensable, the language of Trinity defiantly insists that every child is made in the image of 'One God: three persons-in-community.' On each person rests God's unique blessing and deep calling. Our DNA, God's design on our lives, is not to become isolated disengaged humanoids but rather to be participants in the unceasing movements of freedom, solidarity and energy which best express 'life in God' and 'life in the world as God intends it.'

Our hope is to glimpse the holiness of God, not to control the mystery of God

Talk about God always finally needs to give way to communication with God. The language of worship is more than personal—it is intensely relational. This means that in regard to the Trinity our attention is as much directed towards the movement of relations between the persons of the Trinity, as it is to defining the identity and functions which distinguish the three persons of the Trinity.

The movements of freedom, solidarity and energy within the life of God provide us with an important clue concerning the overarching shape and content of Trinitarian worship. The structure and content of the constituent parts (music, prayer, art, storytelling) are capable, within these movements, of generating many kinds of theme and variation. This kind of dynamic improvisation is exactly what we should expect in worship when the source and end of all praise is a God who is love in relationship.

God does not run a closed shop; the Trinity is not an exclusive club. God constantly moves outwards, from the foundation of the world, to create what is other, and yet is of God's self. The missionary nature of the triune God is open, expansive and inclusive. Our life in God is about continuing the processions of God by reaching out in love, offering community, healing and hope in the middle of fragmentation and exclusion.

Notes

1   *Open to Judgement: Sermons and Addresses by Rowan Williams* (DLT, 1994) p 173.
2   Gail R O'Day, *The New Interpreters Bible* Volume IX (Abingdon Press, Nashville, 1995) p 494.
3   Paul Fiddes, *Participating in God* (DLT, 2000) pp 11-12.
4   *Ibid* p 46.
5   Walter Bruggeman, *Theology of the Old Testament* (Augsburg Fortress, 1997) p 563.
6   Bernhard Anderson, *The Living World of the Old Testament* (Longman, 4th ed, 1988) p 494.
7   *Ibid* p 495.
8   Guardian Newspaper January 9th 2003.
9   John V Taylor, *The Go Between God* (SCM, 1972) p 48.
10 Paul Fiddes, *Participating in God*.
11 Steve Turner, 'The History Lesson'.
12 Rowan Williams, 'Making it Strange: Theology in Other(s') Words' in Jeremy Begbie(ed), *Sounding the Depths* (SCM) p 24.
13 The Cappadocian Fathers were Basil of Caesarea, his friend Gregory of Nazianzus and his younger brother Gregory of Nyssa. They came from the Roman province of Cappadocia, and their trinitarian teaching was especially important in the early church.
14 Paul Fiddes, *Participating in God*.
15 Michael Hawn, 'Form and Ritual: A Comparison between Sequential and Cyclic Musical Structures and their Use in Liturgy' in Helen Phelan (Ed.) *The Breath of God—Music and Spirituality* (Irish World Music Centre, University of Limerick Veritas, Dublin, 2001) p 37
16 *Baptist Praise and Worship* (Oxford University Press) 442.
17 Graham Kendrick.
18 Robert Stephen research.
19 Michael Hawn, 'Form and Ritual.'
20 David S Cunningham, *These Three are One—The Practice of Trinitarian Theology* (Blackwells, 1998) pp 125-129.
21 BCC Report *The Forgotten Trinity* (1989) Vol 2 p 5.
22 Geoffrey Wainwright, *Worship with One Accord—Where Liturgy and Ecumenism Embrace* (Oxford University Press, 1997) p 246.
23 Ruth Duck and Patricia Wilson-Kastner, *Praising God—The Trinity in Christian Worship* (Westminster John Knox Press, 1999) pp 25ff.
24 *We Believe in God—The Doctrine Commission of the Church of England* (CMP, London 1987)
25 Jim Forest, 'Through Icons' in Jeremy Begbie (Ed), *Beholding the Glory* (DLT, 2000) pp 91-93.
26 Alexander Schmemann, *For the Life of the World* (SVS Press, 1998) pp 29ff.
27 *Ibid*.
28 Sam Richards, 'Doing the Story' in Pete Ward (ed), *Mass Culture—Eucharist in a Post-Modern World* (Bible Reading Fellowship, 1999) p 123.
29 Rowan Williams, *Resurrection: Interpreting the Easter Story* (DLT, 1982) pp 75-76.
30 John V Taylor, *Go Between God* (SCM, 1972), p 48.
31 Paul Fiddes, *Participating in God*.
32 Michel de Certeau, *The Mystic Fable* (University of Chicago Press, 1992) p 229.
33 Letty Russell, *Church in the Round*.